A First Look

JESUS

Lois Rock

Illustrated by Carolyn Cox

Educational consultant: Margaret Dean

A LION BOOK

Bible passages mentioned in this book:

1   Luke, chapter 1, verses 67 to 79.
2   Matthew, chapters 5 to 7.
3   John, chapter 6, verses 1 to 14 and 25 to 59.
4   John, chapter 4, verses 1 to 41.
5   John, chapter 15 verses 1 to 17.
6   John, chapter 14, verses 1 to 7.
7   John, chapter 10, verses 1 to 10.
8   John, chapter 10, verses 11 to 16.
9   John, chapter 8, verse 12 and chapter 9, verses 1 to 7.
10 John, chapter 11, verses 1 to 25.
11 Luke 23, especially verse 34.
12 Luke 24, especially verses 4 to 5.
13 John, chapter 14, verses 16 to 17 and chapter 16, verse 7.

Text by Lois Rock
Copyright © 1994 Lion Publishing
Illustrations copyright © 1994 Carolyn Cox

The author asserts the moral right
to be identified as the author of this work

Published by
Lion Publishing
850 North Grove Avenue, Elgin, Illinois 60120, USA
ISBN 0 7459 2497 2

First edition 1994

Rock, Lois, 1953–
        A first look at Jesus / Lois Rock
        ISBN 0-7459-2497-2
        1. Jesus Christ–Biography–Juvenile literature. [1. Jesus Christ.] I. Title.
    BT302.R675 1994
    232–dc20 94–9705 CIP

Printed and bound in Singapore

Contents

Introduction
Who is
Jesus?

One of the first things
that people learn about Jesus
is that he is
the Christmas baby.

Some people believe
that Jesus was a very special person:
God's Son.

Jesus lived about 2,000 years ago.
But ever since, people have heard about
what he said and did
and have wanted to follow him—
to be Christians.

Now there are many, many Christians
all around the world.
Christians believe that Jesus came to show
people how they could be friends with God.

The New Testament part of the
Bible includes stories of his life
written by four different people:
Matthew, Mark, Luke and John.

In this book you will discover some of the things they
tell us:

- about Jesus' birth

- about the things he did and
  the things he said

- about his death—and his
  coming alive again

- about his promise of
  kind of life for anyone
  believes in him

1 Let's look at
Dark times

Do you ever wake up early when the world outside is dark and scary? You wait eagerly for the very first sign of light to show that day is coming.

Sometimes, when things do not go right, you may think that daytime feels as gloomy as night.

That is how the people called the Jews felt two thousand years ago in Israel.
God seemed far away from them, and foreigners, the Romans, had conquered their land. But they believed God would send someone to rescue them.

Just a little while before Jesus was born one of his relatives, Zechariah, said this:

*"God will send
the one who will rescue us . . .
it will be like the sunrise
after the darkness."*

From the book Luke wrote about Jesus

God sent special messengers—angels—who said that this someone was Jesus: God's son. They said so to his mother Mary, to her husband, Joseph, and to shepherds on a hillside.

**Jesus' birth was like the first light of dawn.
People believed he would grow up to make their sad, dark world bright and joyful.**

2 Let's look at
Happiness

When you do something
that you know is right
you feel happy inside.

Jesus knew about happiness.
He grew up with his family.
He played with other children
when he was little.
When he grew older, he learned
the family trade and became a
carpenter.

Then, when he was a man,
he began a new kind of work.
With a few special friends,
his disciples, he traveled around
telling people about God.

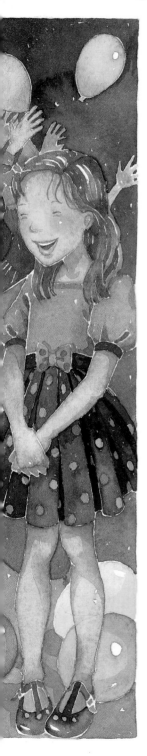

He told them how they could be really happy by living as God wants:
showing love and kindness to everyone,
even enemies;
not staying angry
but sorting out quarrels;
not trying to get revenge,
but doing good;
not worrying about how to get rich,
but helping those in need,
not pointing out other people's mistakes but being sorry for their own mistakes.

Jesus said:
"The people who live in the way that God wants are truly happy."
From the book Matthew wrote about Jesus

Jesus taught people how to live as God wants, so that they will be truly happy.

3 Let's look at

Being hungry

Think how hungry you feel when a meal is late...
When it comes at last you eat and eat.
Then you're so full you can eat no more.
But in a while you're hungry again.

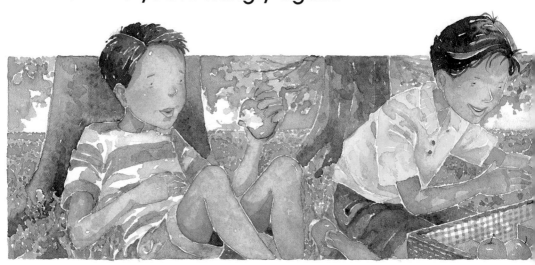

One day, thousands of people came
to listen to Jesus.
But they had not brought any food to eat.
A little boy had brought his lunch along:
five round, flat loaves and two small fish.
Jesus thanked God for this food,
and God made it into enough for everyone.
Jesus' disciples shared it with all the people.

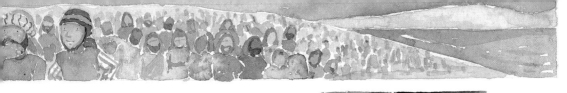

But Jesus said
that tummies full of food
aren't all that people need.

*"There is another kind of food
that people need even more.
God wants you to believe in me—
because God has sent me
to give you life that will last for
ever.
Then you will never again feel
hollow, and empty, and lost."*

From the book John wrote about Jesus

Believing in Jesus is like having a meal—
and the good feeling lasts and lasts!

**Jesus said:
"I am the bread of life."**

4 Let's look at
Being thirsty

Think of a hot summer day:
you have been playing for hours
and now you need
a long, cool drink.

In Israel, the country where Jesus lived,
it is hot and dry all summer long.
One day, Jesus stopped by a well.
He asked a woman who was there
to pull up a bucket of water
so that he could have a drink.

And then he said
that he could give her special water to drink
and she would never be thirsty again!
   The woman was very surprised
because Jesus didn't have a bucket.
He explained
that when people long to be friends with God
it is like longing for a cool, refreshing drink.
Jesus said that he could help her
to be friends with God.

From the book John wrote about Jesus

**Jesus said:
"I can give you life-
giving water."**

5 Let's look at
Trees in blossom

Trees in blossom
look so lovely...
you want to cut off
bits of branch
and take them
home.

But the flowers soon die
when they are cut off a plant.
If you leave them growing
they will keep growing,
and produce seeds and fruit.

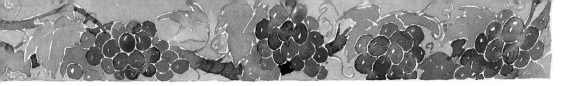

In the country where Jesus
lived there were fields of vines
which produce grapes.
And he was thinking about
how they grow when he said
this to his friends:

*"The people who believe in me
are like branches on a vine.
If you belong to me,
just as branches belong to the
trunk and the roots,
then you will grow and flourish
like a branch that produces lots
of fruit.
But if you break off from me
then you will be like a useless
branch
that dries up and dies."*

From the book John wrote about Jesus

Jesus said: "I am the real vine."

6 Let's look at
Finding your way

Have you ever stepped off the
path you know
and gone off on your own.
It seems exciting to explore
somewhere new...
but what happens if you can't
find your way home?

In the beginning,
the Bible says,
God made people who
would know him
and be his friends.
But instead they wanted their
own way
and lived selfishly.

Jesus told his followers
that he was going to make
a new home for people
where they would be with
God again.

"But where is that place?"
asked a friend called Thomas,
"and how can we know the way there?"
    Jesus said:
"I am the only way
that will take people back to God
to be with him for ever."

From the book John wrote about Jesus

Jesus said: "I am the way."

7 Let's look at
Gates

Think of running to your home...
Will the gate be unlocked
so that you can open it quickly
and go in to where you are
safe?

Jesus said that people long to
be with God,
to be safe with him
and to live as he wants.
But how can they get to God?

Jesus said:
"I am the gate
that will take you to God.
You will be safe with him,
as sheep are inside a
sheep-fold."

From the book John wrote about Jesus

Jesus said: "I am the gate."

8 Let's look at

People who protect us

If someone is taking care of you
it's good to know
that they won't run off
if things get scary.

The shepherds in Israel
in the time of Jesus
had to protect their sheep
from all kinds of danger.
But if a wolf came by
and things looked dangerous
a bad shepherd might run off.

The good shepherd
would stay and protect his
sheep even if he had to risk
his life to save them.
Jesus said that he would
take care of people
just as a shepherd takes
care of sheep.

Jesus said:
"I am the good shepherd.
My sheep are the people
who follow me.
I know my sheep,
and my sheep know me.
I will look after them really
well.
I will even die for them."
From the book John wrote about Jesus

**Jesus said: "I am the
good shepherd."**

9 Let's look at
Light

Light is great:
you can see what you're doing
and where you're going.

Sometimes people who were blind came to Jesus
and he gave them back their sight:
wonderful daylight
instead of a world of darkness.

But Jesus said
it wasn't only blind people
who were in the dark.
Often, people can see well with their eyes
but they don't really understand
what they're doing
or what's going on around them.
It's like living in the dark.
What people really need to see
is what God wants them to do.

Jesus said
that the things he said and did
were like a light
that would show them.

Jesus said:
"I am the light of the world.
Whoever follows me
will have the light of life
and will never walk in
darkness."
From the book John wrote about Jesus

Jesus said: "I am the light of the world."

10 Let's look at
Being alive

It's so sad when living things die
and you know they are gone
for ever.

One day, people came to Jesus
and told him that his friend, Lazarus,
was very ill.
Would he please come and heal
him—
just as he had healed many others?
But when Jesus reached the place,
Lazarus had already died and was
buried in a stone grave.
His family and friends were crying...
And then Jesus brought Lazarus
back to life.

Jesus said:
"I am the one who gives life
even though there is death.
Whoever believes in me will live
even though their body dies."
From the book John wrote about Jesus

God gave Jesus the power
to do a very special thing
that day to show people
that death is not the end,
because God is stronger
than death.

Jesus said: "I am the resurrection and the life."

A new start

When you've made a real mess
how can you begin to put it right?
If only someone loved you enough to do that for
you, so that you could make a fresh start.

The Bible says that people have made a mess of this
world because they do selfish things.
Jesus came to show them a better way
and to put things right.
He showed love and kindness to people
so that they could see how to live as God wants.
But this made some people angry:
they didn't like him telling them what God wanted.

Then one of Jesus' friends, Judas Iscariot, let him down.
He told the people who were angry with Jesus where they could find him alone.
They came and took him away to Pontius Pilate, the Roman governor of their country.
They told lies about him
to get him into trouble.

So Jesus was put to death like
a criminal:
nailed to a cross of wood—
crucified.
Jesus did not argue.
He was loving and forgiving
even as he suffered.

Jesus said: "Father, forgive them, for they do not know what they are doing."

From the book Luke wrote about Jesus

When Jesus died on a cross, he showed them that God loves them and and offers

12 Let's look at

Incredible news

Sometimes you hear news
that just doesn't seem possible.
You'd never believe it
unless you'd seen what happened.

The Roman soldiers put Jesus to death.
Then Jesus' friends took his body
and hurriedly buried it in a grave.
A day passed.
Then early the next morning
some of his followers went to the grave.
To their amazement
the huge stone that had blocked the entrance
had been moved aside.
They went inside the grave...
and the body of Jesus had gone.

*Two people in bright
shining clothes were there.
They said: "Why are you
looking in a tomb
for someone who is alive?"*

the book Luke wrote about Jesus

Later the same day,
and many times
for forty days afterwards,
Jesus' friends saw him.
They talked with him,
and shared meals with him.
They saw the marks of the nails
in his hands and feet.
God had brought him to life again—
death had been beaten.
Jesus' resurrection is the promise of
life with God for ever.

**God brought Jesus back to life, and showed that
he is indeed the life that death can never beat.**

13 Let's look at

Special friends

Little children
often long for friends
who could help them feel brave and strong.

Imagine having a *real* friend
to help you in all you do.

Forty days after Jesus came back to life
he said goodbye to his friends,
and he went home to heaven.
His friends were there when it happened.
But Jesus made a promise to his friends:

Jesus said:
"I will ask God
to send you a special Helper,
who will stay with you all your life.
The Helper is called the Holy Spirit,
who will show you what is right and true.
It's better for you that I go
so that the Helper will come instead."

From the book John wrote about Jesus

The coming of this Helper meant that Jesus could be with them for ever, no matter where they went. Jesus also promised that one day he would come back and take his friends to be with him for ever.

Jesus went away from this world — but God sent his friends the Holy Spirit to help them live as God wants until he comes again.

Let's look at Jesus

Jesus' birth was like the first light of dawn.

Jesus taught people how to live as God wants, so that they will be truly happy.

Jesus said: "I am the bread of life."

Jesus said: "I can give you life-giving water."

Jesus said: "I am the real vine."

Jesus said: "I am the way."

Jesus said: "I am the gate."

Jesus said: "I am the good shepherd."

Jesus said: "I am the light of the world."

Jesus said: "I am the resurrection and the life."

When Jesus died on a cross, he showed them that God loves th and forgives them, and offers them a new start.

God brought Jesus back to life, and showed that he is indeed t that death can never beat.

Jesus went away from this world — but God sent his friends Spirit to help them live as God wants until he comes again